These Things I Will Take with Me

These Things I Will Take with Me

Poems by Carmen Germain

Cherry Grove Collections

© 2008 by Carmen Germain

Published by Cherry Grove Collections
P.O. Box 541106
Cincinnati, OH 45254-1106

ISBN: 9781934999219
LCCN: 2008933134

Poetry Editor: Kevin Walzer
Business Editor: Lori Jareo

Visit us on the web at www.cherry-grove.com

Acknowledgements

The poems in the section *Living Room, Earth* were collected in a chapbook of the same name (Pathwise Press, 2002).

Crab Creek Review
"Writing a Sympathy Card to My Cousin's Wife"
"Chinese Box"
"April, Seattle to Missoula"

Crosscurrents
WCTCHA
"They Want You To Believe"
"February 1913"
"Heart"
"Cold-Barn-Waiting"
"Alone"

Duckabush Journal
"Elisa, Thinking of Winter"

Cold Mountain Review
"The Sisters"

Pontoon
"The Journey of the Saints and Strangers"

The Kerf
"Fire with Fire"

Poems and Plays
"Picking Huckleberries"

Midwest Review
"Something Lost"

Proposing on the Brooklyn Bridge:
Poems about Marriage
(anthology, Grayson Books)
"Injection"

Hurricane Alice
(reprinted in anthology *In a Fine Frenzy:*
Contemporary Poets Respond to Shakespeare)
"Literature 100"

The Sow's Ear Review
"Infinite Jest"
"Known Elements"

Jeopardy
"The Fox Feeds His Death"

The Madison Review
"Not Me"

The Front Range Review
"Winter Pears"
"Daily Bread"

Freshwater
"The Invention of Light"

The Old Red Kimono
"In the Middle of My Life"

Tidepools
"These Things I Will Take with Me"

The Alembic
"Amplitude"

The Tulane Review
"Nothing Gold"

Heliotrope
(in slightly different form)
"They Take Us on a Perugina Tour"

Talking River Review
"*La Ratta di Europa*"
"How They Came to Spain"

Into the Teeth of the Wind
(reprinted in *The Hurricane Review*)
"Pietà"

Flyway
"Fragment"

Natural Bridge
"Monody"

Bathtub Gin
"Fossil Record"
"Work Like This"
"Blue Book"

With love and gratitude to Laura Fox for a friendship in two centuries.

For Tom

Table of Contents

I. Living Room, Earth

Writing a Sympathy Card.................................15
They Want You to Believe..............................16
Elisa, Thinking of Winter...............................17
Trajectory..19
February 1913...20
The Sisters..21
Chinese Box...22
Heart..23
The Journey of the Saints and Strangers........25
Fire with Fire..27
Picking Huckleberries......................................29
April, Seattle to Missoula................................30
Doctor Witness...31
Something Lost..32
Injection..34
Literature 100...35

II. These Things I Will Take with Me

Infinite Jest...39
Known Elements..40
Cold-Barn-Waiting...41
The Fox Feeds His Death................................42
Snow Day on Hurricane Ridge.......................43
Blue Book..44
In the Middle of My Life.................................46
Daily Bread...47
Invention of Light..48
Winter Pears...49
U-Pick, Salt Creek, Washington.....................50
Afterwards, Going through Photographs......51
Dark House at the End of the Road...............52
The Pocket Safety Plan....................................53
What I Saw Today..54

Killing the Monkey..55
Once I taught Literature of War....................56
On that Bus...58
News from Our Place.......................................59
Not Me...60
These Things I Will Take with Me................61
Monody: Visitors Center,
    Olympic National Park..................................62
Amplitude..63
Nothing Gold..65
Work Like This...67
Fossil Record..68
What Dreams Far Away...................................69
School of watching how...................................70
Anniversary, War...71
Last Year, Kispiox Valley..................................72

III. *Pietà*

You Won't Remember......................................77
Infinity..78
First Wilderness, Yosemite, 1972....................79
"Ancient Winter"...80
The Not-God..81
They Take Us on a Perugina Tour..................82
Come Si Dice/How Do You Say......................83
Pantoum: Window,
    Ponte delle Torri..84
Pompeii..85
North and South, Perugia Train Station........86
La Ratta di Europa..87
How They Came to Spain................................88
Pietà...89
Fragment..91

I. Living Room, Earth

Writing a Sympathy Card
to My Cousin's Wife

Deer season and the first snow
of Thanksgiving. My cousin,
handsome and fifteen,
his rifle pointing down the field.
And I am waiting for him to do

something, shoot or lower
the barrel and turn around,
but he stands there
as though he sees
into a mystery I can't know,

girl cousin and young, a pest
who follows the boys on their
hunts, keeping her distance.
He doesn't shoot. He doesn't
turn home either, and I watch

him bound into blue pine shadows,
winter light wavering everywhere.
I know the blood of deer, color
of my father's wool, my brothers',
my uncles'. November sky at dusk.

I wait. Wind cracks the house,
and my mother scours a turkey,
which is desolate, like a naked
baby you wash in the sink.
And all that week a deer cures

in the white pine, tied by rope.
Our leaping dogs nip the delicate
and brittle feet that hang knocking
against the winter bark. I bend
the foot joint, feel motion fleeing.

They Want You to Believe

In the movie, the photographer
for *National Geographic* loves
an Iowa farmwife,
her husband and kids away
at the fair, a wandering man
no woman would choose
when she has her nest
and her sunny morning kitchen.

But when her family's back
and her lover leaves,
she's in the truck with her husband,
hair tightly rolled, pure woman
of sorrow, nipples scorched
where the other took them in.

But even my mother, in a good
Catholic marriage, tells her
Go with him when people clap
in the dark movie theater
as the woman drops her hand
from the door handle, defeated,
the scene cutting to the future,
grown daughter and son
learning truth of naked mothers,
how they open like roses, like fire.

Elisa, Thinking of Winter
—after John Steinbeck

All night I dream
"Quick puffs of colored smoke"
but awake I forget this blooming
close to earth, this thinking
I am beautiful when I am dying.

Red and yellow and purple,
as big as dinner plates
where I bring my hunger,
Chrysanthemums know my hands
and welcome them, like children.

And I told a man not my husband
about my arms and spine,
bone and muscle strong enough
to crack the planet,
to tumble all living things
back into light.

A man not my husband
who lives rhythms of night and moon.
But he is gone, that man:
and I have betrayed
only myself.

But while feasting is all around,
I look at my husband, and he lives
thin.
Scrapes his chair
and goes to prod
slow-faced Herefords
that do not know
they are living.

Hauls hay to horses,
rides fences,
counts pullets.
Tramps each blade of grass
against a small, gray stone.

But he is a good man,
and I grow old,
all my strength brutal
in its summer bloom,
in lacy women's things
that scratch my belly
and breasts
when we go to town
for another dinner
where he will sit thin
even after wine, his mind
snow-filled, thinking
of tractors leaking oil.

And when he wants sex,
he's thin and lean
and works on me like a man on horseback
galloping up the steepest tilt of pasture
needing the valley on the other side,
serene under its burden of fog.

Hoarfrost is the woman
who learns to live alone.
She spreads hands over fields
and does not want anyone.
Yellow summer grass
knows this sorrow
sleeping under ice.
It too wears the bitter lace,
dreams of the mouths
of a thousand feeding things.

Trajectory

The night you brought the gun home
and put it on the table between
red-braided place mats,
it nested in its hard plastic case,
a wedding ring in molded foam.

I'd grown up with guns,
deer season, my father's war,
but this was different.
you told me of those hikers
killed on the Appalachian Trail,
how the man fell into step with them
on a switch back, all alone
except for the birds, so sudden
you couldn't hear air sing.

And I thought of our neighbor
across the road, his rages,
pointing a shotgun
into our woods, shooting
a Deep South of pain,
the kind that breathes fire,
the kind that yanks up close.

Sometimes I hike
a trail when you are gone.
Trees, instead of closing off
light, step apart. Anything
that wants to, can.

February 1913

1.

In the photograph,
my grandmother grips
the farmhouse pump,
black hair soft and unplaited.
Frozen trees crack the horizon,
mute white fields.
My grandfather stands away,
shoulders stiff.
He is cold. He is thinking
of deer.

2.

Her hands stink of milk.
At daybreak and dusk
stanchions shudder
with the bawling from calf pens.
She strokes swollen cows,
leans her body into great hips,
pulls teats toward steaming pails.
Darkness and huge bellies
steady her.

3.

The child dead,
she drains her breasts.
How hard to be like the moth,
who cannot know grief,
whose dry heart's an ornament.

The Sisters

We know they renounce us,
choose to live with women only,
the convent a small compound
across the street from the school.
Renounce children, that is, miraculous gifts
from God, and therefore houses full
of us, and everything that goes with us.

What do nuns know,
gold bands on their marriage fingers,
brides of Christ—

What we know: our parents take naps
on Sunday afternoons, bedroom doors locked,
Patsy Cline or Johnny Cash on the radio.

For us, the world feels like a bus
that'll never come.

Chinese Box

All night I climb in dream rubble,
wind cracking sleep
like a sheet left out on the line.
But this morning is the world again.
East light heats wooden floors,
my long hair winds comb's teeth,
my husband's blue shirt drapes a chair.

They say if you live long enough,
you, too, will live alone, your love
like a Chinese box. Inside the roar
of longing, a great November storm.
Inside the storm, a small, new music.
Inside the music, a wild, red fox.

Heart

I married my first husband
because I thought he had money,
and every night I curved over
his body, my eyes on the pulse
in his neck, waiting for him

to die and open the door. He
was old and arctic, a slice of man,
who used to sit and scowl by
the window, watch me in the garden
tend roses and peas, his mind

not on love, but on food. How
I would pull ripe apples
from orchard trees, taste
bitter desire, boil
their bite and flesh

into seedless foam
so he could gum the mush,
this threadbare stick of man,
how I would tear fruit from branches,
my face covered in leaves!

My second husband I married
because he drew a circle in sand:
We are each half of each.
I felt the sun and moon move
the earth in its orbit,

the belly of a woman full
with child, stones rolling
in rivers, the shape of mouths
kissing. Then I learned
the sea's pulling tide.

His love vanished in one sweep
of earth's swift journey.
When, in passing, a man praised
his own wife to me, I saw how
some women catch love and luck

like stars fill an August lake.
I despised her, whose man in joy
believed *She is my blood,
my green fire, my light,* and
because I could not kill her,

I stole his heart and bit it in two.

The Journey of the Saints and Strangers

> *And the season it was winter sharp and violent.*
>
> —William Bradford
> *Voyage to the New World*

We remember the terrible crossing,
the time we had of it.
Sick for weeks with nothing
but the faces of women
turning in on themselves.
And the nights with no moon!
Our hands peeling blackness
to find nothing.
Dried fish and quarrels
clogging our throats,
and seas mad with rain
spilling our blankets.
And the sharp stink,
the dens where we slept.
And the child born
in the reeking hold,
given the name of the sea,
his mother washing blood
with Leyden water,
weeping for oranges and small birds.

And days we thought we would die,
and remembered stone bridges
and red brick streets,
and wondered why we had come.

On the sixtieth morning
we saw whales' spray.
Strangers cursed,
for we had nothing
to take them with,
and then seabirds
and the seamless land
watching.

Then great trees kneeling
down, the bay so dark
we thought we'd come
to the end of the world,
instead of the beginning.

    –after T.S. Eliot

Fire with Fire

> *Imagine yourself in Hetch Hetchy*
> *on a sunny day in June, standing*
> *waist-deep in grass and flowers...*
> *while the great pines sway dreamily*
>
> –John Muir

You were wrong
about this one thing, old father:
take my neighbor
up there at the podium.
She's gone feral,
reads the great Chinese
nature poets,
has taken to sleeping
in forests, her mantra
the roar of all rivers,
her hair the color of deer.
Today she's pulled on clothes
to be here, brings silver salmon
and birds—paintings—
canvas-blue hope
for no rock quarry
on the riverbank,
which is why we're here
    at the scoping.

But when she quotes Stafford,
>   *Around our group I could hear*
>   *the wilderness listen,*

and then brings you in—
>   *Everyone needs beauty*
>   *as well as bread,* their eyes

roll back in their heads.
Not the sacred moment
you would hope for.
And the attorneys
for the mining company
haven't looked up
for ten minutes.

I too know words
with music
in their shoes.
But old father, last leaf,
it's time to forget all that,
time to stoke
sediment and erosion,
target species and wellsprings,
water tables and extinction.
Time for facts waist-deep
as your June flowers.
But still language
that can break your heart.

Picking Huckleberries

Even when you pull a sack over a bush
and shake hard, they remember anger
and won't drop in your pail.

It's got to be red berry by tedious berry,
holding to the last familiar thing.
How sometimes there's nothing to do

but keep working, like groping in a room
for light, and the night rain drumming the roof,
and someone you want, gone.

April, Seattle to Missoula

When the doe stepped out—
eyes tight on the head beams—
you said your one word
god, and I jolted awake,
and then she was gone.
I remembered that Wisconsin night
when I was a child trying to sleep
in the back seat of the blue Rambler,
Father and Mother talking up front.
How white pine and deer glinted
in and out of light, but more
than this—the way
a moment can change you.

How we came first on the wreck
and I saw the man, then the woman.
As though they had pulled off the road
for talk, his arm slung out the window.
His head thrown back as though
the woman had said something hilarious
as she stared out the shattered windshield.
And the velvet buck broken in the ditch?
He listened carefully, too, his brown
eyes, like hers, slowly emptying.

Doctor Witness

I scoop out the kidney like a plum.
It's dull work, after all.

I've seen them risk the knife,
spend what's left of their lives
kicking their wives,
black sun drinking the fields,
so where's the healing?

Always quite like this:
imagine selling your kidney
because your crops wither.

And a child with his cup of rice
and bone-arms, rags blowing off ribs,
spider webs torn by wind—
and thieves fat. And more born
every day.

My hands suture
a split in the world.
It is finished.

No one hears
a plum drop in an orchard
seven thousand miles away.

Something Lost

      1.

Why do I
wear my hair so long
past forty?

When I was ten, I wanted nothing
on my neck, and so
it was shaved up the nape
and bristly, soft and strange.
But missing the weight
of something lost
I grew it back
abundantly.

The week before I left home forever,
a woman said *Now you look like one of us*,
my dark hair piled on her tile floor,
my face a stranger's.
My uncle saw me on the street,
thought I was a boy.
I liked that metamorphosis,
that trying on of difference.

      2.

I stood on our porch
in Bellingham while you cut just below
my shoulder blades the single braid
hanging below my hips.
Inappropriate, the hair stylist to the rich
and famous said on the talk show,
meaning hair should graze
only the shoulders
of women past thirty,

so I still wasn't doing it right.
And why did women in the audience
clap and cheer when the volunteer's lush hair
fell to the stage floor?

Injection

I follow the nurse's instructions.
Load the hypodermic,
tap for air bubbles,
remember I flunked
chemistry in college.

You clear your throat.
You're like a glass bowl
tipping on the edge of a shelf.

I cup my palm
on your naked hipbone,
one finger pointing at your spine,
make a V, puncture,
draw back from your wince,
check for blood. Only then
plunge into muscle.

The surprise when my body
hums like bees.

I've stabbed too hard.
You cry out, as in sex,
as in nightmare,
but I clench the syringe
and don't flinch, damn all.
We're caught in this together.

How it feels to hurt you—
out of trees something charges,
breath hot on my face,
lopes back to cover.
And I'm lost, rounding
blind curve after blind curve.

Literature 100

Iago had his reasons,
but still we wonder
why he did it—
the fisheries students
who'd rather watch the video,
the engineering major
who calls Desdemona
that sleaze ball,
the nursing student
who keeps saying
*It's all easy, it's all just
   soap opera*—
why he stunned the Moor
with innuendo's rag of grief,
handkerchief with its pure seam
of blood, each thread embroidering
a new womanly sin,
each whisper, each glance
pointing its finger
anywhere but straight,
the cracked-cup universe
    finally put on the table.

II. These Things I Will Take with Me

Infinite Jest

What does he think of his death,
the most powerful man in the world?

Not the spread in *Newsweek* and *Time*
afterwards, the drama he does

or does not believe comes true off stage,
but his actual dying. The moment

when the limo throws a rod,
when Death pulls up in a dented taxi,

double parks, scratches a three-day
beard, goes in where

the most powerful man
is picking his teeth, calls out his name.

Known Elements

When they drop the Bomb,
Mr. Snider told us,
*It won't matter
how pretty your hair is.*

Dust, he said, looking around.
Just like the stars.

I collided with physics
all that eighth grade year—
metals, nonmetals, noble gases—
all weighing in like secret sin.

Sulfur didn't mean brimstone
and wasn't yellow.
A red chair sat black
when you closed the light.

You could knock an ant
out of the same high tree
where your brother fell,
and the ant would run away
on its bent-pin legs,
unlike your brother, bleeding
himself into hard March ground,
incapable of desiring anything.

Cold-Barn-Waiting

The reason I am here:
those horses eating hay
in the snow. Four hours
since I grabbed the wrong keys,
tossed bruised apples
in a bucket of oats, hauled bales
to the barnyard door.

Up the hill our house waits
bloodless and serene, locks
aloof to ignition key
steamer trunk
file cabinet
gas cap key.

You will be gone
a long time,
my greatest fear.

Will meet an old friend in Safeway
and catch the ferry to Victoria
for pot stickers at Three Dragons,
fly to Juneau for the full-mooned,
green-eyed glacier.

Mail postcards from Truk
and Rome and Istanbul,
your last address
a pale-purple orchid.

The Fox Feeds His Death

The fox has trapped
waves in its fur.
See? Wind torments it.
muscle and tooth
are water: salt water,
rain water,
water from all rivers.

Cliffs are where
the fox would like to be.
No stink of rabbit,
no bloodied eye
that looks then leaps away.
only desert, black and remote,
circling the horizon.

Snow Day on Hurricane Ridge

—after a line by Galway Kinnell

Tired of straightness,
sliding waxed skis in line,
my left foot diverges
and my right declines
until I'm angled into deep snow
like a truck gone off the road.

Then out of nowhere
a snow board swings
the steepest grade
and sweeps down slope,
the unseen world tipping.

A kid cutting school,
body slipping loose
as a strand of silk
through the eye of a needle,
setting something free.

God of what comes to pass,
god of what comes—
keep for us this meeting,
underneath this heat
the old hug of earth.

Blue Book: Corner Basin and Bienville, New Orleans, 1906

—And me, oh God, I'm one

See her at night
nowhere a more popular Madame
handsomest octoroon in America
mirror-parlor a dream

nowhere a more popular Madame

aside from beauty, possessing
the largest collection
of diamonds, pearls, and other rare gems
this part of the country

See her at night
nowhere a more popular Madame,

aside from handsome women,
the most costly
oil paintings in the Southern country
mirror-parlor a dream

always something new at Lulu White's
always ten entertainers,
recently arrived from "East,"
well known to the "profession,"
who get paid to do nothing
but sing and dance

    Chloe, Adeline, Minnie
     Hazel, Grace, Billie
      Mira, Fay, Nada

      "Good Time"   Color W.

*An essential guide to the District
because it puts the stranger
on the proper grade or path
as to where to go and be secure.*

In the Middle of My Life

She's wild spring foxglove,
        fireweed, orange tiger lily.

Walking with the evening
        world, she's June's green crop.

How could I keep you from seeing?
        Gold October of crisp light,

my body's an orchard in far-off rooms.

Daily Bread

Waiting in line at the supermarket,
I think of a student's spell-checked paper.

*My dad gets up at 3:00
in the mourning and heads for Seattle
where he works for Safeway
in their whorehouse.*

All those hours slinging freight,
cracking weight of daily bread,
crates of Mexican oranges,
lemons like spilling suns.

The *S* riding his back
like a biting red snake.
How sometimes people say,
I prostitute myself for this job.

Or is the *S*
a river flowing—
milk and eggs and bread—

a trout on a fly when the flood's done,
a kid in college writing essays,
a car that *goddamn starts* and runs?

Invention of Light

The sow heaves with desire,
wishes to bruise her snout
against the wall smelling of dawn,

clump teeth into stone,
topple into sun.
Even a sow, children filling the world,

dreams. Truck-wheel squeal
you think contains pig-brain, dark
slop-intelligence—

hums with faith, sudden sun
on the wall's free face startling
bending light into being.

Winter Pears

All morning black-tailed deer
stab feet through orchard grass
for last pears, sweet-rot
globing at the heart.
Up the mountain the bear mother

and her husband sleep separate
after agreeing
to create the world.

I strip last beans,
dip hands under potatoes.
Soon night blazes
with left-over stars,
and this bright planet
leaving, too.

Something stirs.
The falling of light.
How to take hold:
putting by, maybe, *now*.
Can, pickle, freeze.
Fold silent tendril,
the white bud of ease.

Chained on the edge
of forest, the neighbor's dog
cannot stop barking

U-Pick, Salt Creek, Washington

A family laughs
in the next row,
but I am alone,
a boat that bobs empty
against late summer's dock,
unannounced, without ice
or heat.

They have brought a camera,
pose children, baskets of berries:
*Smile. Show us
what you picked
all by yourselves.*

Once I couldn't wait
to fly my life
out of the Midwest,
plane lifting
from cornfields
and Mississippi,
away from my people,
their distrust of things
not held in the hand.

Now we say goodbye again
and again.
Wild strawberries
bittersweet and spare.
When it begins to rain hard,
the family scatters.
The farmer walks back
from his roadside fruit stand,
offers me
his wife's wide canvas hat.
Here, he says. *This will keep you dry.*

Afterwards,
Going through Photographs

Here he's on an island
off Japan. Sailors crowd the frame,
brothers in the same stew.
You're his son, safe in his wallet.

How you hated backyard baseball,
the war over,
your glove hand steaming
from his fast pitch,
red as the stop signs
between love and love.

How you refused to hunt,
stroking dead rabbits piled in the trunk.
He said *they cried like babies.*

That summer on Glass Lake
he hadn't seen you in five years—
*I'm a stallion,
but you're still a pony—*
that old man fishing, whipping his rod,
furious at the still water,
the graceful line you flashed.

Dark House at the End of the Road

        Dark house at the end of the road,

how alone I am   white, frozen mornings
    when the plow scrapes   the country road

and it is still and dark.   I wait at the kitchen window
    with coffee   and watch lights wind

the hill toward me,   snow silently filling the woods
    while someone I love   is sleeping, is sleeping,
        is sleeping,

and I want to keep the life   in this dark house so still
    nothing will seek it out   nothing will blaze and burn.

Safety Plan Pocket Guide

Stay out of closets.
Avoid kitchen, bathroom, and garage.
Keep shoes next to the bed.
Stay out of rooms with only one exit.
Get a plug-in hot cup. Hide
bread under the bed with your shoes.

In the summer, wash outside where you see
the cars in the street, the house next door. Spray
the garden hose to rinse the soap from your eyes.
If it's winter, don't wash. Learn to love the sweat
under your breasts, the sweet soil of your scalp.
Hide a blanket under the bed
with your shoes and bread.

If you can't leave when it's happening,
when the fist punches the air next to your face,
when the corner of the counter cracks
your spine, when your head's a bird trapped
in a shed, when you say something stupid,
and the words claw the air like a hundred
hungry cats. If you can't leave the room
with no exit, the house next door.

What I Saw Today

Witch, Hag, Baba Yaga—
old women in fairy tales:

you shuffle the black wool evening,
worry the street. The man in the car
next to me heels the steering wheel,
traffic light red and green and red.

Daughter, sister, mother, lover—
history's a door latched for the night,
a number shaped in human light.

I will not say you want to be young,
I will not say you want to be old.

You wait on a street, and like magic,
like seven seas parting,
cars halt on either side—

young woman in a thin dress,
braided copper hair,
golden ball of the world
rolling, rolling, rolling.

Killing the Monkey

You curve over *Reading beyond Words*
like a surgeon studying a belly
before the knife spills
what's hidden.

By our second week, words shift shape.
"Construction" has no –shun.
There's "job application," but to
"shun someone"
 is something else.

It's so easy to stray
from WorkFirst's fill-in-the-blanks
when words break open
like hot bread.

You tell me how in Soledad you bartered
sketches for love letters another man
composed to your wife—
"The words from someone else's heart,"
unlike the roses you drew for her.

How at thirteen you couldn't read
your own story to the teacher,
who imagined your skull
sizzling over a campfire—
"Here we have a specimen of a fried brain."

And how when everyone left,
and you were alone
with the scrawny pet monkey
who kept laughing in its cage,
you strangled it—a kid who loved animals.

—for R.

Once I taught Literature of War

to college students who walked in doors
of recruiting shops in shopping malls,
Children ardent for some desperate glory
or money for college or jobs.

All Quiet on the Western Front
and then we'd return to our concerns,
October's red leaves, the promise
to pay attention.

So what could I say to the boy
who shrugged off the drama of it,
the hand reaching for the butterfly
in the last frame? I think of the sweep
of cedar up a mountain with the sun
burning the frost off the stripped poplar,
how steam this way curls just like smoke.
If I think of a dry August without rain,
I see the wood of my house in flames.
The boy in the movie reaches for beauty,
too, and what draws in, kills.

This other one in front of me thinks
we'll spill blood by computer
in the world of the future,
click by click in blue height
unlike the sky.

They can't help him,
those few men who turn toward light
and leave the mead hall's roaring.

Or the Marine who told me once
all those years ago how no woman
would sleep with him

because of the shrapnel that seared his belly,
then carefully unbuttoned his shirt
and proved it.

On that Bus

He was always on the Nassau bus
whenever you'd catch it for fishing.
Kinderhook Creek, out of the city, your rods
collapsed, Airex Spinster reels, summer.

Nun-free—Sister Theophane,
Pay-NEEN-sue-lah of geography,
Sister Aloysius, "don't"
where you should say "doesn't."
The priest in his red convertible
full of high school boys.

Find rainbows in the riffles
and brookies in the pools
and big browns under snags

You called him Ol' Snags, not cruel,
not where he could hear. Boys free,
clear water dripping from the tip,
the delicious wait for fish to hit.

He was always on that bus,
not knowing he'd tell you,
same advice, every time. Boys fleeing
scum gutters, B-Girls and cops
next to certain cars, fathers home
sweaty, shouting at the radio,
mothers wiping babies.

The same advice, all boys being the same.

Your bus rolling stop signs,
in a hurry to build up speed, watching
behind to know what's coming.

—for Tom and John

News from Our Place

Blue snow drifts over
salal and blackberry cane,

and the silent birds of winter,
that left-over tribe,

riffle the trees for seeds.
That was last week.

By the time you read this,
our tracks no longer answer

when we try to find
where we've been.

Not Me

All your atoms
bolt for a second
then settle down
like starlings landing—
the pickup blares
around the sharp curve,
my friend, just missing.

And the china plate
you left on the burner
by mistake,
glass shards spiking
just as you closed
the kitchen door.

And the downgrade
to the Cheyenne River,
brakes smoking—
U-Haul trailer
shoving relentlessly,
sweeping your car side to side,
through with taking orders.

Just so you know—
in the loose-sock drawer
of luck, things tangle.

These Things I Will Take with Me

First, how you hold
my fingers at night
when we are half asleep
and walls slant over the bed,
sweet briar clawing window glass,
cold wind draining off Mount Angeles.

Then our garden in late August,
its pool of green
sunk in the dry yard's back.
Zucchini flowers' orange fists
and white bean blossoms in the path.
The dark, feeding life of roots.

Next would be this day's morning,
its wild bee luminous and insistent,
and the San Juan's blue haze:
great sleeping turtles.

Last, this starless peace
that waits in the weedy field
and gray-boned shed. Empty.
Remembering nothing.

Monody: Visitors Center, Olympic National Park

So it happens
you fall for a man
you see in a photograph
taken 100 years ago,
caught in this mountaineer gallery
next to plaster tracks of cougar.
He, too, waiting to pounce,
eyes clear capital,
the way they take hold.

His hands buried
in pockets
covering hip bones,
smell of damp wool.
You want to hear him laugh,
and the ache hangs like dust.

But you're in this world.
Men have been before him.
Even children born, wrung
from that hunger.

And you understand fists
full of hair, the smooth
hinge of hip. Love
like all the climates of earth.
But worst—
what he's lost, choosing you.

Amplitude

> *Not an inch nor a particle of an inch is vile*
> Walt Whitman *Song of Myself*

I don't know how to name things
I cannot see. In this Lebanese restaurant,
lush buffet spread on three oak tables—

spinach and onions, pasta as fine as the lines
this pen makes, cucumbers, yellow beans,
yams in their buttery roasting pans,
rolls of rice coated in fruity olive oil
and sesame seeds, she's here, too—

in this former flower shop transformed
by kitchen and ovens, feeding this
street, *Flowers* still on the neon sign.

She struggles to stand, no easy work,
her body planted between herself
and the littered table, crumb-stuck
chair jerking back, belly stranded
with pasta, rivers on a world's map.
It's All You Can Eat.

I look away, think of a mirror in a house
with its face turned aside, a woman
with thighs like baked apples.

She brushes hands streaked with sauce
through hair, and I see the floor,
chunks of tomato scattered
around the island of self.

She turns toward me, a grunt
for what's left, server dumping bread
in a basket, a twist to the bowl of pasta.

Her chins dripping sauce, she hoists
one leg and then the other past me,
flesh bobbing like a fishing boat.

Great-hearted man of all singing
    not an inch is vile

forgive me,
I cannot see.

Great-hearted man of all singing:
in all people I see myself.

Nothing Gold

Exhausted from the red-eye flight,
we don't know where sleep should be.
Back home, the maple's gold buds
and the tongues of rhubarb
have come out with the light.
But here, three thousand miles east,
we've come to bury your mother,
and gray snow still rings the city's heart.

At the cathedral altar, the priest sees
beyond where I can see,
slumped here in the pew.
He means to be kind. When we falter,
mouths shaping the hymn of Christian burial,
he sings louder, trying to carry us through.

From the four directions, tall candles flame.
Incense swirls in brass bowls,
raising apparitions from childhood—
saints gesturing in spiced smoke
the threat of hell,
God chewing on a chicken bone,
and every beach fire with its writhing.

If only I could have been
like St. What's-her-name,
spilling a thousand pins on the plank floor,
picking them up one by one, doing this
penance each day, knees bleeding,
I might have been perfect enough.

Now he's saying the one we love
isn't in the coffin draped
with the simple white cloth.

Isn't: the hymn I hear,
walking toward the wafer,
his steady hand,
knowing well my pagan heart.

Work Like This

For three days the wasp builds
a tight dome, weaving the
eaves above where I sit

on the porch after chores
are finished. I watch it
paint layers of paper.

The nest hole's down, rain
can't flood the cells.
The wasp chews the cedar

of my house. I hear
jaws reaping the wood grain,
ticking in my walls,

my stairs, my fence rails.
Work like this makes more
work. I aim the garden

hose, sorry that killing
comes down to what's
mine, what's yours.

Fossil Record

Five petals in a perfect circle
sink into mud, and I hold

a million years in my hand,
stone's perfect memory

printing its one word.
And lichen, the optimistic

architect, spreads blueprints
on rock. A boy wears

a sweatshirt that says
Now here, and when he

hunches his shoulders,
    Nowhere.

What Dreams Far Away

I dig potatoes, Yukon Gold.
It's Sunday, and you're making *frittata,*
tear basil from the pot
on our window sill, shake from its jar
oregano from the summer garden.
When I bring in the first load,
I hear the crack of beans
as you grind vanilla coffee,
fragrance following me back out
where I lift clumps, hands cold
with October mud. You call me
to bring what else I've found
so we can eat and get going
and get things done:
coat the leaky trailer before rain,
fix the brakes on the truck,
figure medical bills,
find the missing receipt—
pushing, prodding, vanishing day.
You're playing a recording
of loons and wolves and then
a wail the size of a forest,
a loon on a lake in Canada.
Once we watched a sow
and three cubs grazing,
moon sifting spruce,
morning fog streaming
from China Knows Mountain,
I see it still.   We thought
we would always live this way.
I step through the door,
wolves open their throats
to gather what's lost.

School of watching how

it's done: the hard work,
stone scraping hide,
sun high. Each root,

worm and ant, sweet
grub. Each tree, each bush,
each red jewel's juice.

And birds snagging
gnats. And bear tearing
what tries to lie low.

All claws of the world,
digging. Flee or fall,
the bone planet.

Always our hard work
crouching by rivers,
close to the body.

Soft fat we'd roll
on our tongues, feeding,
calling death home.

Anniversary, War

In the Green Leaf Restaurant, the baby girl screams in the highchair where her parents have strapped her. The father leans and pats her arm, the way we touch the very old to comfort them. The child from the next table, fat in his first year, leaves his family to stand by her. Alone among us, he understands the world can vanish if you turn your head. I want to brush my hand lightly over his black crown, the soft heat of his skull. Our story relies on flashback, replicates its one cliché. And asleep in the rain of the world, the one seed, flower or weed. While you read this, a man and a woman make centuries of it.

−after Elsa Morante
History

Last Year, Kispiox Valley, British Columbia

> "September now
> Only a breath of summer remains.
> Uprooted, I stand at this eastern window
> and watch sparrows drift from the maple
> like brown leaves. I own nothing here,
> the eye clear in new air."
>
> Judith Minty
> *Walking with the Bear*

I.

    No wind at all, but the saplings are crazy on the buffaloberry knoll. It's early morning, and we're in the house we've been building, a place for summers. We're behind cedar paneling from our neighbors' land up river. We're behind pink insulation, plywood from Prince George, fir siding we painted one board at a time. How hard we worked then, coating both sides, stacking wet boards on scrap wood we piled in weeds, the man we hired hammering dry boards to plywood, tar paper shredding in the evening wind. How we'd watch weather stain the Babine Range, and we'd work faster.
    Once you pointed at a double rainbow arching the valley. After a stolen moment, we bent back to work. Once a pheasant cock slammed the roof and stumbled through the air. A loon called, leaving Pence Lake, and a coyote watched from the edge of forest. Black flies flew in our eyes, and mosquitoes under our sweat. We quarreled when the man we hired left in his pickup at the end of the day and forgot his little dog. Our solid tree. Floor, metal door, green tin roof. Our rusty van, coated with mud from last week's rain, a mile of ruts to the gravel road. No

easy way out.
    I had that feeling for the first time then. Stomach rising, or a deeper rising, almost sexual. And the acetone fumes you could never smell. And I saw an old man, *who was he?* Our friend who was dying back home? struggling across the floor, back bent, arms dragging down. And my stomach rising, the knowing ahead of time what someone was telling me before the story got going, the fumes no one could smell. How in those moments I knew some gravity deep in my body needed me to stop whatever it was I was doing. I told no one. Would you? But the day came when I was handed a word full of fine bones that caught in my throat.

2.

> *No wind for all the commotion,*
> *and then we see*
> * three cubs of the year*
> *ring out of the bush,*
> *berries on a slot machine,*
> *the grizzled hump*
> *of the sow herding them.*

    She plops down like a Hereford from my childhood, tears off cow parsnip, jaws close to the meadow, face a dish of rock. Placid in the fog, she never swings her head in our direction, keeps feeding, the dark-chocolate cubs watching how.
    At an expensive hospital in the Midwest, they'll drill a hole in my skull, precisely, and slice out something as small as a robin's egg or as immense. Until that time, phenytoin keeps lightning out of my brain, but I weep at a tone of voice, an exasperated sigh. One day we

struggle with a heavy plywood board up the stairs, and you say *turn right, turn left, go counterclockwise, follow me as I spin upside down and tilt the board at a sideways angle horizontally. Don't drop it.*

    For that moment, we watch the bear family forage. Then they rise together and vanish with such ease I wonder how such magnitude moves through the world with such grace. I'm staring at the patch of berries. I'm staring at the fog burning off. But you saw them too.

III. Pietà

You Won't Remember
(A Wish for a Friend)

–after Montale
"La Casa dei Doganieri"

You won't remember the house
on the high bank, strapped

so desolate by evening.
The wind in your rooms.

Freed by dead years,
the sound of your loneliness

will feed a sweet homesickness.
You won't remember, but in the distant

house and in disguise, memory will be
a soft patch of green you'll lie in.

Light ascends in a straight line.
Is it here? But people always break apart.

You won't remember this evening house,
and who goes and who stays.

Infinity

   –after Leopardi

Always you'll return
to this silence,
the horizon's locked gate.

Unending mirrors
and the sovereign silence.
You'll know your body, your eyes,
your fear before the wind.

And how wind storms
between infinite space
and death's seasons,
your small life.

In this immensity
You'll be glad of sleep
in your own sweet sea.

First Wilderness, Yosemite, 1972

    –after Ungaretti

In our beginning,
we held no terror of virgin rivers,
implacable ruins of great, fallen trees,
the broken angles of the rigid.

This is what we want to think.
But this valley haunts our future's
perfect magical apparitions:

the river-music, the quiet granite,
della natura estrema la tensione,
the extreme tension of nature,
what's kept, what's let go.

"Ancient Winter"

    –after Quasimodo

You want pure work
and the hope of spring,
and then you'll die,
ancient winter.

When you carve
birds of snow
and first words of sun,
that ragged angel,

then damp rim
of stone and forest
face the air's morning.

The Not-God

> –after D'Annunzio
> *"La Pioggia nel Pineto"*

The rain in the pines. Listen.
Above the woods, no word.
Rain drips branches, needles
and bark, rain the long pages
of pines, the listening fern and vine.

It does not know our song.
It does not know the beautiful past
we invent. Do not bow
before the great bear,
the fearless birds,
the rain in the pines.

Under innumerable fingers
of rain is the clear creature,
sea and earth. Its song
makes room for us,
little by little.

They Take Us on a Perugina Tour

and afterwards, we loaf and joke
and listen to the textbook English

of the beautiful sales boy Bacchus
we'd like to bed, who gives out *Baci*

with clichés printed on paper ribbons—
To Live Without Love Is Long Death.

Gold *Baci* kisses, milk chocolate cappuccino,
chocolate-covered Toschi cherries, white fudge,

Torrone Mandorla, bittersweet chocolate almonds,
and the *Gran Amore* of all, the boxed treats

richer than pearls. And in the factory museum,
TV commercials from the 50's, selling it.

One ad keeps looping. A suitor, Perugina
for his girl, teases open her mouth,

and her breasts spin to milk chocolate,
and her nipples swirl to knobs of crème.

Then fade-out *sotto voce,*
and how we imagine him swallowing her.

Come Si Dice/How Do You Say

In this *pasticceria* they're a day old,
and we're sure they're soggy,
try to say "fill now?" and "make fresh?"

We've forgotten *il dizionario,*
buying sweets for tomorrow's breakfast.

It's late afternoon, and the pile's low—
Neapolitan cakes, crusty bread,
and what we want: *cannoli.* We point
at golden-rolled scrolls, *ricotta*-stuffed,
the Vegas stripper Sugar
in bed with the accountant Cheese.

The woman explains and explains.
Ci sono freschi! Fresh, fresh, fresh!

We know slow swirl of confection
and candied orange peel,
one large bar of sweet chocolate
chopped in the bowl just before,
just when it's right,
ricotta spooned
without cracking the shell,
the crisp jacket of fried dough.

What curls down
the other tongue and sleeps,
what keeps us from her now.

How she stands in the doorway
wailing goodbye or cursing,
hand open or about to slap.

Pantoum: Window, *Ponte delle Torri*

Where night steals up
like a black-hooded monk
the wind's a fist
sealing the ravine.

Like a black-hooded monk
puts finger to lips
sealing the ravine,
someone's left marigolds,

puts finger to lips.
This is the place
someone's left marigolds.
The great spiral streams.

This is the place
Be merciful to him in his misery
the great spiral streams
deep pitch, still falling.

Be merciful to him in his misery
prayer propped on wind,
deep pitch, still falling.
The world's a stone,

prayer propped on wind.
The wind's a fist,
the world's a stone
where night steals up.

Pompeii

How was it then, in the avalanche
of night, ash swallowing cooking pots
clogging throats of birds

Black sky spread its skirts
pale women called their children
in the river, fish listened

North and South, Perugia Train Station

*No one has come to this land
except as an enemy, a conqueror,
or a visitor devoid of understanding.
Christ Stopped at Eboli*
Carlo Levi

"*L'italia è bella,* but not Calabria.
Not a good place...not even Italians—
Albanians." This day's gone on too long,
and last night, our bed like rows of teeth.
But she's friendly in a crusty way,
helps us stash our bags, chats in English.

But not in our tourist dictionary—
Terrone, the slur for Southerner.

I ask her why she feels this way.
"Because they lie, cheat, and steal!
Tell you one price, add on more,
make you pay! And women...
they aren't safe in the South."

Before we left home, your uncle told us
it's called the *Mezzogiorno*—
"Land of light, like the sun at noon,
which means 'No better than a dog'
among stupid people."

Once when I was a girl, I hid a sack
of sugar donuts in a secret
tree stump in the woods.
Drunk on sugar,
I didn't see the sweet ants feeding
until I swiped my mouth.

La Ratta di Europa

It's stifling
in the *Uffizi* basement
where I breathe dark corridors
lighted in front of the Masters.
What is rape anyway? Seduction
by bull, plunge into sea,
artist tricking a smile?
I fumble for the brochure's Italian.

She sat in the back row,
didn't come to class the day
we read "Rape Fantasies."
Told me Atwood was a fool.
I explained it's *not* condoning,
can't you see where the woman is?
In a bar, talking down the fear
sitting next to her?
But my student knew.

They stuffed me in a trunk,
took me up a logging road.
When they were done, they left me.
I walked down the mountain
naked.
And out of another century, someone
wrote Leda's myth, and paintings
with Europa: "When one sees her
loveliness, one can't help
envying the swan."

The gallery rides out the end of day—
women on backs of serpents, bulls,
horses, camels—and the lovely Europa,
smiling astride Jupiter, maids
pitching with her into deaf, green sea.

How They Came to Spain

> Otello Ricci
> 1904 - 1938
> *è morto nel*
> *cielo di spagna*

Otello in Hell with the other Othello,
the other one who believed
everything he was told.

I like not that, Il Duce said,
and you're going to show them.

So Otello went. He flew his Fiat
so the Luftwaffe could keep
its mind on business, like hawks
circling before they drop to kill.

He loved his plane, the sorry box
that barely kept up, and it's true,
there wasn't much to do around here.

Or some worm cored
to his heart and the world
with a hole in it, hollow.

When the post-war books
were written, we all saw
Guernica—how bombs
snapped the village's neck.

And maybe my brother—
under his finger bones
      the claw of machinery.

Pietà

> Marcello Casini, 1931-1944
> *In sequito a incursione aerea* 13 3 '44

1.

Thirteen, Marcello loves to race
the stone streets,
vanishing down alleys
when he sees his mother striding,
her baskets of bread.

> *She'll make me*
> *go with her up hills,*
> *make me tilt my face*
> *toward old women,*
> *their quick, dry mouths.*

He remembers his father
took him to Monteluca,
to the Sacred Wood,
how lost below the town looked,
like hats flung in a pile and forgotten.

Today he runs toward spring,
early and green,
runs alleys until they spill
into the lower part of town,
the train a finger pointing.

2.

We none of us dared say anything, her only child. She told the sculptor Cestino exactly how to do it, and he did. If any dared, they might say she was taking on too much, but she was stronger than any of us. What would you do, your boy brought home to you like that? She must have seen it right away. We all have: the Madonna on one knee, her son just down from that death-wood, his broken body draped across her body, arm hanging down, pointing toward earth, head resting in the broken curve of her. So that's what Maria wanted. Her son held that way, by her, in stone. But his body a child's in the pose of the man-Christ. But a child—and killed by men.

Fragment

Museo Nazionale del Bargello, Florence

How fragile our breath among the rubble,
our human expression of desire,
sun after rain as we follow these streets.

And Bernini knowing this, holds us
here as the woman's coiled braid
loosens, throat bare,
her garment's disarray
pulling us toward our own lives
on days obliged to nothing.

Or *Brutus,* how Michelangelo
chisels him larger than life,
mouth tense with what's broken,
the way we jut into the future
when it can't be changed,
deep in the gut denied
until we no longer deny.
How we live, pushed open.

But against me now,
heat, and stone solid with story.
How can it be that we die?

I look at you—
the one who lies beside me
in the peaceful night,

each rib the root of all calling,
alone, each.

Notes

These Things I Will Take with Me

"Snow Day, Hurricane Ridge": A tribute to the work of Galway Kinnell, an early mentor, whose poems taught me and continue to teach. "I know/ The birds fly off/ But the hug of the earth wraps/ With moss their graves and the giant boulders." Galway Kinnell. "Flower Herding on Mount Monadnock." *Galway Kinnell: Selected Poems*. Boston: Houghton Mifflin Company, 1982. 64.

"Last Year, Kispiox Valley": Judith Minty. "Six Poems for Nine Crows." *Walking with the Bear: Selected and New Poems*. East Lansing: Michigan State University Press, 2000. 124. Used with permission.

Pietà

The following poems were inspired by Charles Bernstein's "Homophonic Translation": "Take a poem...in a foreign language and translate it word for word according to what it sounds like in English....Don't use a dictionary, just rely on what your ears hear and go from there....the results can be surprisingly revealing of unconscious aesthetic and personal proclivities." The results share elements with jazz improvisation; the poems riff on the sounds of the original and then create their own world. Behn, Robin, and Chase Twichell. *The Practice of Poetry*. New York: HarperCollins, 1992. 126-128.

"You Won't Remember": Eugenio Montale. "La Casa dei Doganieri." Rebay, ed. 136.

"Infinity": Giacomo Leopardi. "L'infinito."

Rebay, ed. 104.

"First Wilderness, Yosemite, 1972." Guiseppe Ungaretti. "Tu Ti Spezzasti." Rebay, ed. 126.

"Ancient Winter." Salvatore Quasimodo. "Antico Inverno." Rebay, ed. 144.

"The Not-God": Gabriele D'Annunzio. "La Poggia nel Pineto." Rebay, ed. 112.

Rebay, Luciano. Ed. *Introduction to Italian Poetry*. New York: Dover Publications, Inc. 1969.

About the Author

Carmen Germain was born in rural Wisconsin. She teaches writing and literature at Peninsula College, Port Angeles, Washington, where she is also a co-director of the Foothills Writers Series. *Living Room, Earth* was published by Pathwise Press. Her work has appeared in the anthologies *Proposing on the Brooklyn Bridge: Poems about Marriage* (Grayson Books) and *In a Fine Frenzy: Poets Respond to Shakespeare* (University of Iowa). She has been published in *The Madison Review, Natural Bridge,* and *Heliotrope*, among others.

About the Artist

Quinn Zander Corum grew up on a farm in Minnesota. After high school she joined the Peace Corps and served in India. She finished her B.A. in cultural anthropology at the University of California at Berkeley and lived for two-and-a-half years in Brazil. Oregon has been home for the past twenty-four years. Quinn has work in private collections throughout the United States and British Columbia and in galleries, including the Center for Contemporary Art, Christchurch, New Zealand.

Printed in the United States
124367LV00004B/493-516/P